Han Ulrich Obrist

Indexed

Everything You Always Wanted to Know
(About Curating)

Holly Crawford

This is the second book in which I have used different approaches and methods to understand the text presented in his book and provide an index for the reader for their better understand of this very important curator. The original interviews, that are my source material, are published in his book *Everything You Always Wanted to Know About Curating** by Hans Ulrich Obrist from Sternberg Press, 2011. This book is a page by page list and index, with his chapter heading, of his curating concepts. Obrist's interview starts on page 15. Text before page 15 is from the introduction by Tino Sehgal. All text in this book are only from the responses made by Obrist and not from the person or persons who where the other half of the conversation. Pages without are intentionally left blank. (The watermark of conversations and research is mine.) The blanks are the silence. Obrist thinks silence is important, so do I. How you decide to use those pages is left up to you. Fill them or leave them blank.

This is the second book that I have produced with indexes that use the text from his book. My first book was to produce two indexes of all the names that Obrist mentioned. This book is a list of the art concepts and ideas which he mentioned. Maybe these two projects will be helpful to artists, critics, and art historians. I have created a text portrait of Obrist. It is a guide to him and his projects.

These reductive lists of his concepts, the two indexes and the previous book, are provided as an artistic, educational and scientific project.

Holly Crawford, Ph.D.
March 2015
NYC

BEFORE AND AFTER

Interview with Enrique Walker

hundreds of different issues
chance
improvisation

THE FUTURE IS A DOG

With Markus Miessen

formula project
ongoing
immaterial exhibition strings
recipes
art travel without the object traveling
ideas
dematerialized exhibitions
idea of lists
unrealized projects

my projects
conversations
facilitation of

conversations & research

vacancy
agency
dangers of neo-colonialism
slowness
technological
cultural
demographic shocks
idea of a new feminism
memory

conversation project
research

The Elephant Trunk in Dubai

With Ingo Niermann

research

bring people together
salons for the 21st Century

conversations & research

bridges across disciplines
unrealized projects

Question: What is Art?

schizophrenic situations coexisting in the same situation

research

research

notes
video tapes of everything
review process again and again

large collages
zero-sum calculation
further production
frenetic pace
great amount of content

radical display

new display features
inventing something
dialogues with artists

laboratory exhibition
experimental exhibition
number viewers verses hours viewing
large scale urban laboratory
not about objects
allotted time not space
elimination of wall texts and catalogs
time important

artists allotted time not space
unrealized project
thinks about how scores survive
instructions not the object is the work

finding the moment again
avoiding repetition
every show might be the last
interested in reviving exhausted formats
I want to work with all the formats

immerse myself in the world of science
curating produces ephemeral constellations
no memories of curating
obsession with archive
interviews

overexposure problem
everything began with literature
exhibition art and literature references
intimate exhibitions

videos—1,500 hours of filmed interviews
longing to work like a writer
find new systems
marathon interviews

work with same people for ten or twenty years
learn from mistakes
make mistakes
(same artists)

start thinking
more monumental spaces
time-dependent spaces
discursive spaces
institution processing shocks of differences
all my projects are fragments
museum as repository of time or a laboratory
oxymoronic situation produces very interesting museums
internet only small part in art world
delays are revolutions

no longer sufficient to infiltrate one reality with
another
point is to produce these realities
to infiltrate a museum like a virus
now the point is to invent an institution
my archive of unrealized projects
exhibition contributes to production of reality

The Postman Rings…

With Philippe Parreno and Alex Potts

give artists not space but time
idea of libretto important
need for libretto so an exhibition can be reenacted or restaged
repetition and difference
Cage, open score

not fininite a group exhibition
artist not illustrating curators idea
collaboratively worked out that there will be no film
or video of the time based project
do something live and not mediated by film or video

importance if film, new reality and work of art

A Mad Dinner in Reagan's War Room

With Brendan McGetrick

main work curating but has parallel activities
research and knowledge production
interview project
interview project predates everything
everything stated with conversations
all conversations are working conversations
working on show, conference or book
new projects grow out of conversations
"productions of reality conversations"
obsessed with art
architecture
involve architects in exhibition design

inventive display feature
imagining a city as a performative space
exhibition as a city
laboratory

experiment with the format of exhibition
laboratories
interview practice
interviews together
working with formats
inventing new formats
new formats
interviews

building temporary pavilions
memory
dynamic memory
idea of memory
multiplicity of museums

questioning master plan
self-organization
dynamic systems with feedback loops

protest against forgetting
going against fear of pooling knowledge
going back to my beginnings

collaborations and dialogues
unpredictability of non-linear
design, not too much design
dialogues
models where difference is maintained
not to embrace globalization blindly
important that there is an art world
parallel realities

nonapplicable models important

map out platforms for seismic shifts
nonapplicable model
complex work
complex artists

possibility of an impossibility
history of ideas

producing reality in terms of architecture
exhibitions is actually a city
building a new city as a curatorial project

virtual or actual, intertwined
think about relation to television

The Enemies Art Those Audio Guides

With Jefferson Hack

sustained conversations
changing of locations
conversations
long interviews

(danger of interviews) always the same things
edited writings of major artists
sustained interviews
production of reality
unrealized projects
interviews

idea of self-censorship
unrealized projects
calculated uncertainity and conscious
incompleteness

archive, laboratory
memory
memory
new cities

conversation
promiscuity of collaboration
slow lanes

not only fast lanes
enemies are those audio guides
conversation
always draw diagrams
nonlinear rendering of the conversation

Something Is Missing

for Lucius Burchkhardt with Juri Steiner

interview marathon project
spirit of Situationism
interview, Situationism
psychogeography
interview marathon
against the background of Situationism
interview
psychogeography

psychogeography
neo-Situationist approaches
connection to the political dimension

transposition is as intelligent as the object
parallel realities investigated
not a matter or either/or
information processing

new alliances and new networks

what a movement when there are no longer
movements
what connects the group
impossibility of capturing a city
quasi-capture the impossibility of the possibility

science of taking a walk
psychogeography
psychogeography the crucial point

interview marathon
danger of becoming a brand
idea of mapping
performative space
transform matter into a performative space
concepts such as, drift, diversion, psychogeography, and dissipated strolling
oscillation set in motion
walks take place
interview marathon
contemporary forms of Situationist practices

danger of homogenizing globalization
need for diverse museum models
problem with audio guides
and viewing exhibition in a very linear way

multiple meaning important
museum is a site for the production of knowledge
place of protest against forgetting
a dynamic tool box
zone between past, present and future

I Was Born in the Studio of Fischli/Weiss

with Nav Haq

directly out of conversations
more conversations
do something unspectacular
very intense dialogue
lots of interviews
collaborate
interviews
interviews
interviews in more informal setting

audio recordings
research method
filmed conversations
project is complex dynamic system
feedback loops
Dorner book became by guide
other fields of knowledge

conversations & research

interviewed many architects
exhibitions are knowledge production
linked to memory
allow dialogue
movement against forgetting
different formats
interview subcategories
different kinds of interview categories
different categories of interviews
art interviews
science interviews
architecture interviews
interviews

going beyond fear of pooling knowledge
interview project
cross-fertilization
part of curator's activity is not public
unrealized projects
very long interview
interviews

conversations
liberate time
curating and criticism rather fragile

Italian interviews
Spanish interviews
Russian
French
English
German
Chinese
interviews in languages I cannot speak
interviews in Chinese

interviews happen in different situations
interviews
interview marathon
interview marathon

The Importance of Being in the Kitchen

With Markus Miessen

"what exhibition is necessary?"
my whole work has been based on conversations
infinite conversations
complex dynamic system
demand for interviews

conversations & research

commissioned interviews
interviews with specific people
interviews are like my school
idea of me as an art curator was far too limited
performative space

white cube is only one possibility
invent new spaces
interested in house museums

time codes
superimposition of different time codes
being in between geographies

A Protest Against Forgetting

With Gavin Wade

exhibitions as examples of complex dynamic system
exhibition could be an ongoing conversation
an ongoing conversation is like every show I have been involved
it always starts with a conversation
develops into a new conversations
triggers more conversations
exhibition is a performative space
performative space

dynamic thing of memory
putting things into relationship with each other
private house
discussions triggered
exhibition display triggering a conversation

conversations
came out of conversations
started with a conversation
infinite conversations
out of infinite conversation organize an exhibition
it's always been a conversation

conversations
series of interviews
idea of these interviews
through interviewing
art that could be moved around by visitor
just ideas
reductive white cube ideology

white cube ideology
almost prevented anything else
a museum shouldn't be reductive
different forms of experiences

protest against forgetting
protest against forgetting
interview project
interview project
dialogue
interview projects
interviews
interviewed them again and again

conversations & research

record conversation
artist talk about other artists
interview project
memory element
protest against forgetting

interview project
interview project
interviews

conversations & research

my interview project the whole twentieth century
different interviews
oral histories
oral transmissions
curatorial history

interview
interview
interviews
interviews

interviews

travel
research
interviews
interviews
interview
interviewer
interviewer

post-planning idea
interviews
feedback
interview
interview

24-hour marathon
portrait
interview marathon
partial portrait

interviews
interviews

interviews
unrealized projects
Agency of Unrealized Projects
interview

unrealized project
unrealized
interview

Can An Exhibition Be Collected?

With Noah Horowitz

studied economics, political science, and sociology
bridging gaps

admired the innovative guerrilla productive methods
experiment
conversations

distribution mechanisms
collaboration

challenging conventions
ways beyond objects

research
slow and deliberate process
dialogue
exhibition both inside and outside
exhibitions where they least expect
globalization impacted structure of art market
global dialogues
global dialogue
small shows in big museums

re-inject different temporalities
edit or play
exhibitions are productions
right context
the appropriate loopholes

self-sustaining distribution model
critical mass
inventing organic circuits
book recent manifestation
algorithmic
open score

issues raised
access
transmission
mutation
infiltration
circulation
distribution
learning system
feedback loops
enhance pathways or circuits
offering another art economy

system of possibilities
knowledge production exercise

idea of art as "elite for the masses"
never considered myself to be an artist
close to artist who think
exhibition space as a medium
role of facilitating

exhibition choreography
exhibition as a medium
I am a catalyst

reinvent exhibition formats
valuable role of archiving

conversations & research

collections less about a single object
collections of exhibitions
how non-objects and quasi objects trigger new forms

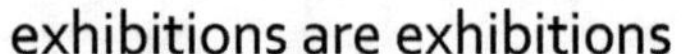
exhibitions are exhibitions

archives capable of sustaining future knowledge production

part with concept of institution as absolute center
conversations

open-source model
being more flexible
status of artwork versus documents

all these floating satellites
home
where the books are

Taxi, Paris, 8-10 pm

With Sophia Krzys Acord

role of curator
long list of duties
protect
facilitator
to create free space
curator as a bridge
build bridges

creation, production, realization and promotion of
ephemeral situations
invent you own trajectory

I like to surprise people
absence of a style is my style
reinventing new sets of rules
curiosity my main constant

exhibition foster dialogues
practice oscillating between order and disorder

exhibition within exhibition
publication is not secondary
publications become primary

buy at least one book a day
want to produce or edit
publishing is not limited to exhibition

research
research is the exhibition
exhibition is research
research
expand notion of curating

be in the middle of things
but not the center
work in waves

It's Alive

With Paul O'Neill

exhibition as a program

'theme' of the show trigger
continuous process of dialogue
emerging collaborations
feedback loops

look at other fields

interviews

time protocol of the exhibition
artist have different time instead of space
trying to reinvent

open-ended
non-linear storytelling
reinvent

interview project

Labomatic

With Jean-Max Colard

nonauthoritarian concept of exhibition
my medium is exhibition

artists have foreknowledge about everything
intuitive
masterminds of the unthinkable
the impossible

routine is the enemy of exhibitions
how to change rules of the game
conversations
art happens where you least expect it

continual conversations
my working method
how can an exhibition develop a life

conversations & research

exhibition asks questions
experimental radicalism too rare

exhibition with irregular dates
research, conferences, and exhibitions
resistance is important
dialogue
Slow conversations
Continual conversations

only email
oscillationg between being connected and disconnected
linking and delinking

era of post-medium
ephemeral

art dialogue
dialogue

If It's Tuesday

With Robert Fleck

dispersal and dissemination
change the rules
make an intimate space

conversations

research
permanent research
research and dialogue

research projects lead to
collaborative projects

ISBN 13:978-0692394595
ISBN 10: 0692394591

Terms, the text listed here, are from the interviews that were conducted by others of Hans Ulrich Obrist and published in 2011.

Text from Hans Ulrich Obrist
Formatted and indexed by Holly Crawford

www.hollycrawford.xyz
www.art-poetry.info

Published by Lokke, NYC

www.ingramcontent.com/pod-product-compliance
Lightning Source LLC
Chambersburg PA
CBHW072134170526
45158CB00004BA/1373
* 9 7 8 0 6 9 2 3 9 4 5 9 5 *